Bear Hugs

•❀ ♥ ❀•

Cheerful thoughts, poetry and Scripture
on love and friendship

Zondervan*Gifts*

Bear Hugs

Blessings of friendship
Each new day
Another bright treasure
Revealed in a smile

For: Peggy

From: Shuuy

There are worlds I've experienced—
Discoveries, no end—
That I'd never have known
Were you not my friend!

Joy MacKenzie, *Friends through Thick and Thin*

Requests for information should be addressed to:

ZondervanPublishingHouse
Mail Drop B20
Grand Rapids, Michigan 49530
http://www.zondervan.com

Senior Editor: Gwen Ellis
Creative Director: Patricia Matthews
Project Editor: Pat Matuszak

Printed in the United States of America
98 99 00 /DP/ 3 2 1

Hours when we
Understand
God's gift of
Special friends

Friendships are the heart's great treasure,
Pearls of price no scale can measure.
Promise of silver, gift of gold
Found in friends both new and old.

I need friends the way I need to garden. I need the challenge of it—preparing the soil, working at the task. Blooms don't just happen, you know! I need the cultivation process—giving it time and attention, learning when to water, when to feed, and when to be patient.

Gloria Gaither, *Friends through Thick and Thin*

In a garden you can hear
God laughing.

Joy MacKenzie, *Friends through Thick and Thin*

Therefore, as God's chosen people,
holy and dearly loved, clothe yourselves
with compassion, kindness, humility,
gentleness and patience.

Colossians 3:12

For those who sing with saints below
Glad songs of heavenly love,
Shall sing, when songs on earth have ceased,
With the saints above.

Godfrey Thring

Maintenance Tips for a Friendship Garden

Forgive easily. Get the chip off your shoulder.

Don't rule anyone out as a potential friend. Sometimes we think a friend has to be "just like me!"

Want to be a friend? Think twice! Strong friendships almost always involve self-sacrifice. People who don't wish to be inconvenienced . . . don't usually endure.

Have friends or die! *America is in the midst of a loneliness epidemic and it's undermining our health. Recent studies indicate that health problems we call "depression" and "low self-esteem" could just as accurately be called "loneliness."*

Joy MacKenzie, *Friends through Thick and Thin*

Man looks at the outward appearance,
but the Lᴏʀᴅ looks at the heart.

1 Samuel 16:7

It is not possible to always be happy.
It *is* possible to always have the joy of the Lord.
Some have described it as a calm centeredness that
tickles at the edges. It's a solid assurance that laughs
if given the chance. It is unwavering confidence
that can't help but look on the bright side.

Joni Eareckson Tada

Our mouths were filled with laughter,
our tongues with songs of joy. Then it was said
among the nations, "The LORD has done
great things for them." The LORD has done great
things for us, and we are filled with joy.

Psalm 126:2–3

Fun is a mystery that can't be trapped like
an animal or caught like the flu. It comes
without bidding if you have eyes to see it.
Learn to find fun in unlikely places.

Barbara Johnson, *The Joyful Journey*

A cheerful heart is
good medicine.

Proverbs 17:22

A friend loves at all times.

Proverbs 17:17

Research tells us that if you're a talker, you'll choose a willing listener as a best friend. Boy, are they wrong!

Joy MacKenzie, *Friends through Thick and Thin*

The joy of the LORD is your strength.

Nehemiah 8:10

Think of all the things that make up
the joy of the Lord, and your smile
can't help but last. My friend Tim Hansel
once said that joy is peace dancing.

Joni Eareckson Tada

Each daybreak is a gift to us
sent from heaven above.
Each sunset is the Earth's amen
to God's great gift of love.

Remember when you were a kid, lying on your back
in the grass, discovering pictures in the clouds?
Remember how you and your "best friend ever" would
often see the same object? That's the way you *knew* she
was your best friend ever. You saw things alike!

Peggy Benson, *Friends through Thick and Thin*

Beauty and grace are performed whether
or not we will (them) or sense them. The least we
can do is try to be there. We must somehow take
a wider view, look at the whole landscape.

Annie Dillard, *Pilgrim at Tinker Creek*

The story of God's love for mankind in the Bible begins and ends in a garden; from Eden to Gethsemene to the Resurrection and even in the new heaven and earth of Revelation—God and man have met together in the cool shade of gardens.

Whom have I in heaven but you?
And earth has nothing I desire
besides you.

Psalm 73:25

God is love.

1 John 4:8

Now Jesus is no porcelain prince,
  His promises won't break.
His holy Word holds fast and sure,
  His love no one can shake.
So if your life is shattered
  by sorrow, pain, or sin,

*His healing love will reach right down
and make you whole again.*

Joni Eareckson Tada

No one has ever seen God;
but if we love one another,
God lives in us and his love is
made complete in us.

1 John 4:12

The commandments . . .
are summed up in this one rule:
"Love your neighbor as yourself."

Romans 13:9

A real friend believes in the real you,
even when you doubt yourself.

The hands of God will hold us close
in ways that no earthly friend ever could. You have
a Father . . . Lover . . . Friend. . . . and Home in
heaven. God is as near as you'll allow Him to be.

Mary Pielenz Hampton, *A Tea for All Seasons*

"I will be a Father to you, and
you will be my sons and daughters,
says the Lord Almighty."

2 Corinthians 6:18

How great is the love the Father has lavished on us, that we should be called children of God!

1 John 3:1

We learn to recognize the seeds
of friendship from those modeled by
our parents and other adults (and)
from our childhood experiences.

Gloria Gaither, *Friends through Thick and Thin*

Ruth Graham boasts of a sign in her kitchen
that reads, "Divine service conducted here three times
daily." When everything becomes a token of God's love,
you feel as though you possess everything. Our duties
are sweet when seen as service to God.

You see a kitten wrestling
with a sock and giggle over
God's sense of humor.

Joni Eareckson Tada

You catch grace as a man fills
his cup under a waterfall.

Annie Dillard, *Pilgrim at Tinker Creek*

In many ways we are like the lost Alice in Wonderland, being stretched and pulled in different directions as we travel through the dark tunnels of life, but then we see a hint of order, a sense of who we are. If we look closely with our souls, we discover God's imprint on our hearts.

Christopher de Vinck, *The Book of Moonlight*

Only that day dawns to which we
are awake. There is more day to dawn.
The sun is but a morning star.

Henry David Thoreau

God who is love . . . simply cannot
help but shed blessing upon blessing
upon us. We do not need to beg,
for He simply cannot help it!

Hannah Whitehall Smith

Dear children, let us not
love with words or tongue but
with actions and in truth.

1 John 3:18

Kind words, warm hearts
And trust that's earned
Is friendship's start.

I am often gently nourished by
a friend whose quiet company provides
wisdom and comfort for my spirit.

Joy MacKenzie, *Friends through Thick and Thin*

Whoever loves God must
also love his brother.

1 John 4:21

A real friend makes a difference
in your life, without choosing
your path for you.

Let the peace of Christ rule
in your hearts, since as members
of one body you were called
to peace. And be thankful.

Colossians 3:15

Friendship . . . is a rare gift,
but it's not without cost.

Sue Buchanan, *Friends through Thick and Thin*

If I speak in the tongues of men and of angels, but have not love, I am only a resounding gong or a clanging cymbal.

1 Corinthians 13:1

A real friend calls you just to say hello
and doesn't give up if the line's busy.

With the help of the Gardener, we can begin to
have a little something bloom in our lives—something
simple and beautiful, like a new friendship.
Something that will help us to take heart on
the days when the storms come.

Gloria Gaither, *Friends through Thick and Thin*

Let the word of Christ dwell in you richly
as you teach and admonish one another with all
wisdom, and as you sing psalms, hymns and spiritual
songs with gratitude in your hearts to God.

Colossians 3:16

Friendship is like a prism through which the many variations of beauty are revealed in our lives.

Follow the way of love.

1 Corinthians 14:1

Love does no harm to
its neighbor. Therefore love is
the fulfillment of the law.

Romans 13:10

Jesus Christ created a model of love, as He did of friendship. We hear from His heart the welcoming words, "I have called you friend." Mind-boggling!

Joy MacKenzie, *Friends through Thick and Thin*

The difference between believers
and unbelievers: it is not that one group
never hurts and the other group does.
The difference lies in what people
do with their hurt.

Christians who long for a better country, a heavenly one, are convinced that one day something so glorious will happen in the world's finale that it will suffice for all of their hurts.

Joni Eareckson Tada

Forgive whatever grievances you may have against one another. Forgive as the Lord forgave you. And over all these virtues put on love, which binds them all together in perfect unity.

Colossians 3:13–14

A real friend invites you to come in
even when the house is messy.

It's only with the heart that one can see clearly. The most important things are invisible to the eyes.

Antoine De Saint-Exupery, *The Little Prince*

It is with your heart that you believe.

Romans 10:10

We need not set out in search for a friend . . .
rather, we must simply set out to be the friend
Christ modeled—anticipating the needs of others,
wearing ourselves out at giving. . . . The rewards
are infinite and joyous!

Joy MacKenzie, *Friends through Thick and Thin*

Whatever you do, whether in word or deed,
do it all in the name of the Lord Jesus,
giving thanks to God the Father through him.

Colossians 3:17

Let love and faithfulness never leave you; bind them around your neck, write them on the tablet of your heart.

Proverbs 3:3

When you love someone, you naturally want
to do things for them that will bring them pleasure.
God loves us so much that he has given us
thousands of flavors to enjoy, and gardens of colorful,
scented flowers to bring us pleasure.

Terry Willits, *Creating A SenseSational Home*

Both friendships and new seedlings are usually
tougher than we think and miraculously seem to survive
the ignorance and error of the naive gardener. Gardens
and friendship both thrive on warmth and light.

Peggy Benson, *Friends through Thick and Thin*

Someone once said that the
excellency of a soul can be measured
by the object of its love.

Joni Eareckson Tada

We are rich because, as the highest
of God's creation, He gave us the ability
to love back, to return the affection. It is almost
as great to be able to love back as it is
to know you are loved.

Gloria Gaither, *Friends through Thick and Thin*

May your joys be deep as the ocean,
Your sorrows as light as its foam.

The lessons of friendship—patience; self-sacrifice; how to create fun out of frustration; persist with others through all kinds of trials; . . . enjoying the good times; persevering through the bad—laid the foundation for a joyful succession of enduring relationships.

Joy MacKenzie, *Friends through Thick and Thin*

The LORD appeared to us in the past,
saying: "I have loved you with
an everlasting love; I have drawn
you with loving-kindness."

Jeremiah 31:3

Christ's love compels us.

2 Corinthians 5:14

The key to friendship . . . is being able
to accept each other unconditionally. If we can do
that, the rewards are neverending! It's a proven fact we
will stay young longer, are less likely to be depressed,
and will save a fortune in counseling fees!

Sue Buchanan, *Friends through Thick and Thin*

Only love can be divided endlessly
and still not diminish.

Anne Morrow Lindbergh

The LORD delights in those
who fear him, who put their hope
in his unfailing love.

Psalm 147:11

If I had to narrow the secret of . . . friendship to one thought, it would be that *we bless each other,* and within the blessing is a kaleidoscope of meaning—to make happy, to praise, to thank, to protect, to sanctify, to favor, to celebrate, to give benediction.

Sue Buchanan, *Friends through Thick and Thin*

By the word of the LORD were
the heavens made, their starry host
by the breath of his mouth. . . . The earth
is full of his unfailing love.

Psalm 33:6, 5

May you find friends wherever you go,
And happily live while here below.
May you prove faithful, kind, and true
To all your friends and they to you.

Minnie Sidders

You are a letter from Christ, . . .
written not with ink but with the Spirit
of the living God, not on tablets of stone
but on tablets of human hearts.

2 Corinthians 3:3

We who are willing to be used also impart
a legacy of Christ's love in the lives of those
we encounter. As the old saying goes, "You may
be the only Bible someone ever reads."

Mary Pielenz Hampton, *A Tea for All Seasons*

We continually remember before
our God and Father your work
produced by faith, your labor prompted
by love, and your endurance inspired
by hope in our Lord Jesus Christ.

1 Thessalonians 1:3

The warming hearth of friendship
is built just one brick at a time.

Seeds are the symbolic heart of friendship—
unassuming, even drab, indistinct contents
of paper packets. Little hopes that are waiting
to be nurtured to full bloom.

Gloria Gaither, *Friends through Thick and Thin*

A real friend loves you
as you are—and as you
dream to become.

Christian friends appear as side paths
we thought we chose ourselves, only to find
we have come to God's destination in our lives
because we happened upon them.

Upon your heart like paper white,
Let none but friends presume to write;
And may each line with friendship given
Direct the senders' thoughts to Heaven.

Time cannot bend the line
which God hath writ.

Henry David Thoreau

It is the earnest prayer of one who
believes that leads to answers.

Charles H. Spurgeon

Best friends are those with whom the give-and-take is joyful and genuine—people with whom I can be my whole self, hiding neither warts nor marks of beauty, and with whom selflessness is never a chore.

Gloria Gaither, *Friends through Thick and Thin*

A real friend loves you for who
you are but tells you the truth
when you need to hear it.

The proper office of a friend is to side with you when you are wrong—Nearly anybody will side with you when you are right!

Mark Twain

We are not friends for fashion's sake;
We are not friends for fame,
But so that we remembered be
When someone speaks our name.

I know lots of folks who are exceptionally
generous givers but so bloomin' self-sufficient
that they would die before they let a friend return
a favor. A good friend is also a gracious receiver!

Gloria Gaither, *Friends through Thick and Thin*

To every thing there is
a season, and a time to every
purpose under the heaven.

Ecclesiastes 3:1 KJV

Love penetrates the defenses that have
been built up to protect against rejection
and scorn and belittlement, and it sees
life created by God for love.

Eugene H. Peterson

My first friend was my mother. . . . She taught me
my first lessons about friendship by being my first, last,
and most enduring friend, and even though she is gone
from this earth, she is far from gone from my life.

Gloria Gaither, *Friends through Thick and Thin*

When the golden sun is sinking,
And God's sweet night begins to fall,
When of absent friends you're thinking
Breathe a prayer for one and all.

Why would God make a flower that blooms
for only one day? On the daylily's part, it doesn't
seem worth the bother. On God's part, it is—
if only to show me, just me, I'm worth it!

Sue Buchanan, *Friends through Thick and Thin*

The nature of moments is so ordained
That time once spent cannot be regained.
Each daybreak comes laden with joy or with sorrow
But ends before sunrise of each new tomorrow.
In the golden chain of friendship,
Each new link has its charm.

One of my favorite early spring flowers is
the johnny jump-up. . . . They remind me that I have
some wonderful *jump-up friends* in my life—people
who have come into my life . . . at just the exact
time I needed to see a friendly, smiling face.

Peggy Benson, *Friends through Thick and Thin*

Daffodils and tulips
Impatient underground
When March sent up a crocus
To take a look around.
Said the crocus, "It is winter!

There's frost on everything!"
But a passerby who saw her said,
"A crocus! It is Spring!"

Author unknown, *Friends through Thick and Thin*

Love is a gift sent from on high
To unite souls as one
And make sorrow fly.
Hold dear as a diamond
The gift from above;
To make life worth living
Just follow God's love.

Life is a process and . . . each of life's experiences—the pain, the glory, the heartaches, and the triumphs—are all part of soul growth. To God, process is not a means to a goal. Process is the goal of life that keeps us moving closer, always closer to an intimate friendship with Him.

Gloria Gaither, *Friends through Thick and Thin*

There I will give her back her vineyards, and will make the Valley of Achor a door of hope. There she will sing as in the days of her youth.

Hosea 2:15

We shouldn't deny the pain of what happens in our lives. We should just refuse to focus only on the valleys.

Charles Swindoll, *NIV Living Insights Study Bible*

The love of God is not mere sentimentality; it is the most practical thing for the saint to love as God loves. The springs of love are in God, not in us.

Oswald Chambers

My heart trusts in the LORD, and I am helped. My heart leaps for joy and I will give thanks to him in song.

Psalm 28:7

A bountiful garden—and a life, open and receptive to friendship—both are sanctuaries for all seasons. The sum of them brings to our lives a glorious melange of color, texture, and form at once reminding us of our roots, enriching our present, and giving purpose to our future.

Sue Buchanan, *Friends through Thick and Thin*

Speak with grace and be
heard with mercy.
Blessed is the influence
of one true, loving human
soul on another.

George Eliot

He who sows courtesy reaps
friendship, and he who plants
kindness gathers love.

Basil

If we find we are too busy for friends,
we must conclude we are too busy.

Sue Buchanan, *Friends through Thick and Thin*

*Bright lie the autumn leaves
Along your path today.
May your blessings be as bright
And never fade away.*

God has said, "Never will I leave you; never will I forsake you." So we say with confidence, "The Lord is my helper; I will not be afraid."

Hebrews 13:5–6

Low at His feet lay thy burden of carefulness,
High on his heart he will bear it for thee,
Comfort thy sorrows, and answer thy prayerfulness,
Guiding thy steps as may best for thee be.

William F. Sherwin

Loving and being loved—being connected,
valued, befriended, cherished by another—
is a compelling need that permeates the life
of every human being on God's earth.

Joy MacKenzie, *Friends through Thick and Thin*

A real friend keeps you close at heart,
even when you are far away.

Thy love is such I can no way repay;
The heavens reward thee manifold, I pray.
Then while we live, in love let's so persevere,
That when we live no more we may live ever.

Anne Bradstreet

However mean your life is, meet it and live it; do not shun it and call it hard names. It is not so bad as you are. It looks poorest when you are richest. The fault-finder will find faults even in paradise. Love your life.

Henry David Thoreau

God loves us with tough love . . .
and that's the way we need to learn
to love each other.

Anne Ortlund

Jesus says that you are
His friend if you do two things:
Love God and love others.

I must remember, Lord, that when I fail as
Your friend, You still remain a faithful friend to me,
always caring and loving, always forgiving and
encouraging. May I reflect Your love back to You
and share that same love with others.

Joni Eareckson Tada

A real friend forgives your mistakes and doesn't remember to be offended.

What is the use of repining—
Where there's a will there's a way.
Tomorrow the sun may be shining
Although it is cloudy today.

I. W. Wiles

Remember friends when far away;
Embrace those who are near.
Cherish those who are your friends,
Forever and sincere.

The longer I live the more convinced I become
that real wisdom and real intelligence and true
greatness belong to us only when we get big enough
to become as a little child and believe in a Jesus
who can make a difference in the way we live.

Gloria Gaither, *Friends through Thick and Thin*

May your life have just enough clouds
to make a glorious sunset.

May happiness be thy lot,
And peace thy steps attend.
Accept the tribute of respect
From all that call thee friend.

T. W. Caldwell

Into any ordinary day, the grace of friendship may break through with unexpected gifts as bright as any rainbow.

Friends are people and people are not always faithful and kind. Just look at some of the people Jesus called his friends: Peter was always interrupting, Mary failed as a housekeeper, indecisive Thomas never stood up for his opinions, and Nicodemus was a chicken afraid to show his face with Jesus in the daytime.

These people had their problems. Nevertheless,
Jesus valued them as friends. He didn't expect them
to be perfect; He expected them to be themselves,
and all He asked of them was their love.

Joni Eareckson Tada

Why should we be in such desperate haste to succeed, and in such desperate enterprises? If a man does not keep pace with his companions, perhaps it is because he hears a different drummer. Let him step to the music which he hears, however measured or far away.

Henry David Thoreau

Friends and family are a treasure from this life that we may keep in the next.

Jesus didn't present a long discourse on friendship. He showed. He demonstrated it by being available, compassionate, self-sacrificing, and tender. His chosen friends responded!

Joy MacKenzie, *Friends through Thick and Thin*

Our search for God and His search for us meet
at windows in our everyday experience. But we
must learn to look with more than just our eyes
and listen with more than just our ears.

Ken Gire, *Windows of the Soul*

Blessings abound—look around you. The smiles
of children, the beauty of a glorious sunset, the comfort
of a warm bed at night. Small and great, there are
plenty of reasons to say to God, "Thank you."

Joni Eareckson Tada

Nature is made to conspire with
the spirit to emancipate us.

Ralph Waldo Emerson

Need help bringing laughter to life? How long has it been since you played the way children do? Simple things like jumping into piles of autumn leaves, or gathering big armfuls of lilacs and taking them to friends' homes so they will smell like spring. Look for fun.

Barbara Johnson, *The Joyful Journey*

There is [a] very good reason for finding a belonging place among a group of believers. I found in my belonging place a place to be needed, to be wanted, and to be loved. A place to be connected to others and to God. It brings purpose and meaning to life.

Peggy Benson, *Friends through Thick and Thin*

Have you entered in through the narrow gate of Christ to abundant and eternal life? When you do . . . Christ will walk with you every step of the way. He is not only the gate that leads you to the Father, but he is also the gate all must pass through who touch your life.

Patsy Clairmont, *The Joyful Journey*

The LORD is my strength
and my shield.

Psalm 28:7

In the world of spiritual pursuits, sometimes
we don't even realize what we're thirsty for. Yearnings
deep within drive us from one relationship to another
looking for fulfillment. There are so many substitutes.

Stop your search. Christ is the real thing.
Nothing and no one satisfies the soul as Jesus
does, for He fills every craving.

Joni Eareckson Tada

As the deer pants for streams
of water, so my soul pants for you,
O God. My soul thirsts for God,
for the living God.

Psalm 42:1–2

It seems to me that everyone, simply, wants to be loved. . . . So it is love—ultimately the love God demonstrated with the gift of his Son—that transforms the abandoned child into a new citizen of the forgiving world, the mother world, the universal embrace.

Christopher de Vinck, *The Book of Moonlight*

If the while I think on thee, dear friend,
All losses are restored and sorrows end.

William Shakespeare

There are mysteries of grace
and love in the Bible: it is a thriving
soul that finds the Book of God
growing more and more precious.

R.C. Chapman

What a comfort to know that in every circumstance
Jesus cares. He cares about each of us. He goes before
us and with us and behind us, providing a soft shoulder
to lean on, loving arms to buckle ourselves into, and
ample light to illumine the dark roads ahead.

Luci Swindoll, *The Joyful Journey*

Intercession (in prayer) is a way
of loving others. We are shifting our
center of gravity from our own needs
to the needs and concerns of others.

Richard Foster

A hand on the arm as we speak or an arm
around the shoulders . . . Appropriate use of touch
can be more important than words. It can say
things that words cannot easily say.

Margaret Gill, *Free to Love*

So let us love, dear Love, like as we ought
Love is the lesson which the Lord us taught.

Edmund Spencer

Through the Lord we are enabled
to let go of our tightfisted hold on life
and follow our best prayers.

Richard Foster

It is the simple things of life that make living worthwhile, the sweet fundamental things such as love and duty, work and rest and living close to nature.

Laura Ingalls Wilder

We can do no great things—
only small things with great love.

Mother Teresa

Our happiness or misery
depends on our dispositions and
not on our circumstances.

Martha Washington

"Stay" is a charming word
in a friend's vocabulary.

Louisa May Alcott

God loves each of us as
if there were only one of us.

Saint Augustine

May the God who gives
encouragement give you a spirit
of unity among yourselves.

Romans 15:5